Original title:
The Chill of Winter Nights

Copyright © 2024 Creative Arts Management OÜ
All rights reserved.

Author: Maya Livingston
ISBN HARDBACK: 978-9916-94-566-7
ISBN PAPERBACK: 978-9916-94-567-4

Secrets Prepared by a Frigid Night

Beneath the stars, the snowflakes twirl,
My nose is red, my toes in a whirl.
The frost bites hard, like a puppy's tease,
Wrapped in blankets, I'm forced to sneeze.

The cocoa's hot, but so is the mug,
I dare not sip, it's like giving a hug.
Snowmen abound, all wearing my scarf,
Last seen chuckling, they'll cause quite a laugh.

The wind howls loud, it's a wacky tune,
Squirrels dance 'neath the pale-gray moon.
I toss a snowball, it lands with a splat,
Right on my buddy, who retaliates back!

In frostbitten shoes, we stomp and we shout,
The laughter echoes, there's no room for doubt.
With every slip, we giggle and glide,
On this frosty night, what a silly ride!

A Realm Where Frost Meets Silence

In the land where snowflakes dance,
Even penguins prance in a trance.
Hot cocoa spills, oh what a sight,
As squirrels plot their snowball fight.

The trees wear blankets, snug and tight,
While snowmen model, looking quite light.
A snowball lands, it starts a brawl,
And giggles echo through it all.

Muffled Footsteps in the Deepening Cold

Puddle jumpers slip and slide,
Snow boots soon become a ride.
Laughter rings through frosty air,
As snowmen lose their hats with flair.

A hot dog van serves soup and cheer,
As kids debate who's the best deer.
Giant snowmen, made with glee,
Can't hold their heads up, let's agree.

Time Stood Still in a Winter Dream

Where time forgets to move and breathe,
You'll find a place where dreams achieve.
An igloo shaped like grandma's chair,
Where each breath forms a frosty air.

The dogs in sweaters strut with pride,
In this cool land, no need to hide.
A snowflake lands upon my nose,
Oh, winter, you certainly amuse us so!

Trails of Frost on Wistful Paths

Trudging through a shimmery glow,
Feet sink deep, oh what a show!
A penguin waddle seems the way,
As laughter leads us through the fray.

Carrots serve as noses, who knew?
Adventures found in chilly dew.
With every step, the silliness grows,
In this wintry wonder, joy overflows.

Chasing Ghosts of Warmth

In blankets piled high, a fortress stands,
I battle drafts with ice-cold hands.
The heater's a myth, a legend untrue,
As penguins parade in my living room too.

Each mug of cocoa's a desperate cheer,
Against the cold bites that draw ever near.
I ponder my fate with a marshmallow plump,
While squirrels plot schemes from their frosty stump.

Sleepless under Winter's Spell

I lie awake, the night is too long,
Counting sheep that sneak off in a song.
The wind howls a tune, a lonesome duet,
While my bed's become a chilling vignette.

There's ice on my nose, a white fuzzy cap,
I'd trade it for sun, a warm sunny nap.
But here I remain, a bundled-up mess,
Dreaming of summer, oh dear, what a stress!

Twilight's Bitter Embrace

The twilight drapes in a frosty shroud,
As laughter echoes from under the cloud.
Snowflakes fall, they dance with glee,
While I slip and slide like a bumblebee.

My ice skates squeak with very loud flair,
Occasionally becoming a bumbling bear.
Friends gather round, oh what a sight,
As I comically biff into the night.

Frostbitten Memories

Nostalgia nudges like an icicle pin,
I recall warm days, where have they been?
Each frosty evening makes my tea a foe,
Yet my absent tan makes me feel like a pro.

Remembering summers with laughter and cheer,
Now switched to snowball dodging out here.
In the game of cold, I unwittingly play,
While dreaming of options like beach holiday.

Chasing Shadows in a Crystal World

In a landscape so icy and bright,
Snowflakes dance, a whimsical flight.
Frogs in boots, a snowman spree,
Waddle and giggle, just wait and see.

Snowball fights with sleds in tow,
Elves in scarves, putting on a show.
A penguin slips, what a sight!
Giggles echo through the night.

Enchanted Stillness Under the Stars

Stars twinkle with a cheeky grin,
As frost-nipped noses poke from chin.
A reindeer prances, lost in thought,
While snowmen wear the hats we bought.

The laughter of children fills the air,
While kittens tumble without a care.
Napping hedgehogs, dressed in flair,
Sharing blankets with snowflakes rare.

Frost-Laden Dreams and Distant Chimes

Dreams of cocoa swirling with cheer,
Gingerbread houses, oh so near!
Bells jingle with a shaky hand,
As winter romps across the land.

Turtlenecks snug, but socks askew,
Frosty noses in a lovely hue.
Hot pies cool while giggles rise,
Who's got the best pie? A sweet surprise!

A Night Draped in Glistening White

Glistening white like a marshmallow treat,
Squirrels in hats, what a funny feat!
Snowflakes spell out silly wishes,
While penguins play in flurry of swishes.

Twinkling lights, a frosty dance,
Frogs making snowballs take a chance.
Worn-out boots and snowy clumps,
Chasing laughter through the winter jumps.

Nightfall's Icy Breath

As the sun sneaks away, the cold goes on,
My teeth chatter tunes like a silly song.
I must take a sweater, oh what a fuss,
Yet I still wear shorts, who's making a fuss?

Snowflakes drift down like tiny lost cats,
They tickle my nose, they dance like acrobats.
I slip and I slide on the frosty ground,
What a hilarious sight, I know that I've found!

Glacial Moonlit Stillness

The moon beams down on the frozen expanse,
While penguins in pajamas begin to prance.
Hot cocoa's a hug for my shivering soul,
But it turns into ice, oh well, that's my goal!

My nose is a beacon, a Rudolph delight,
My gloves are mismatched, quite a fashionable sight.
I waddle like a duck, in boots oh so big,
Winter's fashion statement: look like a twig!

Whispering Pines in the Frost

The pines giggle softly, wearing white caps,
While squirrels play catch with their frozen snacks.
I bring out my sled, but it's missing a wheel,
What a comical scene, oh what a raw deal!

Snowmen are frowning, their noses on freeze,
They long for some warmth, oh please, not a tease!
I give them some carrots, a smile they get,
A frosty embrace, I'll never forget!

A Blanket of Frosted Minutes

Time slips away like a snowflake in flight,
I glance at the clock, it's now past midnight.
My hot soup's a icicle, spoons frozen in place,
Laughter bubbles up, what a funny race!

The blanket of frost seems to tickle and tease,
Every crack in the sidewalk says 'please take it easy.'
So I roll in the snow, like a playful pup,
Winter's a hoot, let's go, fill our cup!

Crystalline Tranquility

Snowflakes dance in frosty air,
A snowman sighs, 'Life's not fair.'
Icicles hang like crystal spears,
While squirrels hide their nuts in cheers.

The ground is slick, let's all take bets,
Who'll fall first and earn their pets?
With every slip, there's laughter loud,
As boots make prints, we feel so proud.

Awakened by the Stillness of Night

Under blankets piled up high,
A snack attack brings a twinkling eye.
The cat's a ninja in the dark,
While outside dogs go mad and bark.

The creaks and groans of winter's tune,
Make me glad I'm not a raccoon.
Hot cocoa spills; well, what a mess!
Laughter echoes—who needs rest?

Frosted Reflections on Glass

Windows frosted, faces peer,
Mittens warm, we share a cheer.
The world outside is cold and stark,
But inside is where the fun hits spark.

Hot air from cookies fills the room,
An oven war, like baking doom.
Muffins rise, and big pies flop,
At least there's seconds—let's not stop!

Veil of Chill

Breezes whisper, tiptoe light,
As marshmallows fight for their right.
In the frosty air, kids start to shout,
Snowball wars are what it's about!

With noses red and cheeks aglow,
We race down slopes, but oh, so slow!
Each tumble's a giggle, each fall's a cheer,
As we toast marshmallows, our laugh's sincere.

Flickers of Firelight Amidst the Frost

The flames dance high, like some wild show,
While snowflakes twirl in a clumsy flow.
Hot cocoa spills, oh what a sight,
As marshmallows dive in, quite a bite!

The logs crackle with a sassy sound,
A squirrel joins in, flopping around.
With a hat too big on his furry head,
He laughs at the fire, then scurries to bed.

The embers wink like stars on the ground,
While toes turn pink with a silly sound.
We giggle together, warmth all around,
In this frosty arena, joy can be found.

A silly dance in the glow so bright,
We jump and we jive, oh what a delight!
As long as the fire keeps flickering flame,
This wintery fun feels whimsically tame!

Charmed by the Bitter Air

With every breath, we puff like steam,
A frosty chorus, what a team!
Woolly hats bob, snuggly and bold,
Laughter erupts, we shiver with gold.

The biting breeze tickles our cheeks,
As we tell jokes in funny peaks.
Icicles hang like awkward chandeliers,
While we dance around, confronting our fears.

Snowmen are built with a goofy grin,
A carrot nose, where do I begin?
Top hats too big, a scarf just as wide,
Together we giggle, can't let fun slide.

Ice skating slips turn into a race,
With comedic tumbles—a laughable chase!
In the bitter air, we frolic and play,
Finding warmth in laughter, come what may.

Hushed Pathways Under Starlit Grey

Under a blanket woven with stars,
We tiptoe softly, avoiding the cars.
With each crunch of snow, we're giggling still,
In our clunky boots, oh what a thrill!

The moon peeks down with a wink and a grin,
As we stumble along, losing our kin.
'Where did you go?' one calls out loud,
In this powdery wonder, we feel so proud.

Snowflakes land on our noses with glee,
Like tiny fluffy gifts, oh can you see?
We strike silly poses for pictures tonight,
In the glow of soft light, we feel so right.

Our paths may be hushed, but laughter's our song,
In this frosty ballet, we laugh all along.
As we silently squeal under starlit display,
Winter's a playground where we want to stay!

Moonbeams on a Frozen Lake

Moonbeams shimmer on the icy sheet,
We slip and slide, oh what a feat!
Face plants galore, laughter's the game,
As we waddle around in the moon's soft flame.

The cold air tickles, what a bizarre feel,
Like frozen feathers or a gigantic meal.
Skates on our feet, we whirl and we twirl,
While giggling urchins give summer a whirl.

Twisted up like pretzels, we take a spin,
With arms flailing wildly, let the fun begin!
Our cheeks are rosy, our hearts are light,
On this frozen stage, we frolic in delight.

When the moon's a spotlight, we dance like pros,
With winter wardrobe, the fashion just flows.
For in frosty lands, fun meets our fate,
Under moonbeams bright on an ice-covered plate.

Secrets of the Frosted Forest

In the woods where shadows play,
Squirrels wear their hats all day.
Snowflakes dance and birds just quack,
A frozen pond holds no ice pack.

The trees have coats of fluffy white,
Raccoons sneaking, what a sight!
A freeze-dried frog on a branch sings,
While the rabbit dreams of springtime things.

Snowmen gossip, trading tales,
While penguins try on tiny scales.
A polar bear with shades so bright,
Steps on ice, but oh! What a fright!

What secrets does this forest keep?
Giggling owls who dare not sleep.
With laughter wrapped in layers tight,
Even winter can't dampen their delight.

Night's Velvet Blanket

As stars peek out to play at night,
The moon has dressed in silver light.
Frogs wear scarves, it's quite a sight,
And owls hoot jokes with all their might.

The chilly air makes noses red,
While cozy cats curl up in bed.
Across the yard, a dog does bark,
His tail wagging in the dark.

Under blankets, children dream,
Of cocoa sips and bright moonbeams.
Snowflakes fall like tiny treats,
Adding fluff to doggy feet.

What mischief does this night bestow?
The mischievous wind sings high and low.
With giggles wrapped in moonlight's glow,
Laughter dances with the snow.

Whispers of Winter's Breath

The wind is talking, can you hear?
It tickles noses, brings us cheer.
Snowflakes tumble, making quite a scene,
On ice skates, all the squirrels dream.

With carrot noses, snowmen pose,
Waving at kids who wear big clothes.
Frosty laughter fills the air,
As children giggle without a care.

A penguin slips, oh what a sight!
While rabbits hop with pure delight.
The whispers wrap the forest tight,
Creating fun from day till night.

Behind the trees, a snowball fight,
With giggles echoing, oh what might.
In this frosty, fun-filled breath,
Even the cold can't steal our zest.

Crystallized Thoughts in the Dark

The stars above are frozen blobs,
Light bulbs out in the chilly sobs.
As penguins shuffle, tripping 'round,
The laughter echoes, joy is found.

A snow hare jests, "What's that I see?
A snowball? Come, let's start a spree!"
But slippery slips, oh what a crash,
Their frosty fun goes with a splash.

In the night, the moon's a friend,
It giggles soft, but will it mend?
The icy paths may trip the toes,
Yet find the joy where warm hugs glow.

With crystals bright that twinkle low,
The night is filled with funny flow.
Through every flurry, laughter sparks,
In this winter wonderland of quarks.

Flickers of Light in the Distance

Snowflakes dance and whirl around,
Like tiny fairies from the ground.
We bundle up in layers thick,
And hope we don't turn into a brick.

A snowman's hat sits slightly askew,
He looks quite dapper, who knew?
But when he melts, oh what a sight,
A puddle in the moon's soft light.

The carols echo from the nook,
We sing off-key, but that's our hook.
The cocoa's gone, the mugs are bare,
But laughter lingers in the air.

So gather close, let's share a cheer,
For frosty fun is finally here!
A winter's night, with glee we shout,
We'll not remember the frigid drought.

Frosty Adventures Under a Glistening Moon

Sleds racing down the hills so steep,
With giggles echoing, not a peep.
But wait! Who's face-planted in the snow?
Oh look, it's just old Billy Joe!

The snowmen all have quirky styles,
With carrots for noses and silly smiles.
A snowball fight breaks out in glee,
But whom to aim for? You or me?

Hot cocoa spills, oh what a mess,
But we just giggle, we don't stress.
A snowflake lands upon my nose,
It tickles softly, then it goes.

Underneath the stars, we dance and slide,
The funniest moments, we cannot hide.
Zooming home, we can't feel our toes,
But in our hearts, the laughter flows.

The Lullaby of Ice and Time

The clock strikes eight, but we're still in play,
Who needs bed when it's a snow day?
With blankets piled high, a fort we build,
The dog sneezes loud, our laughter filled.

The night grows cold, the moon's aglow,
While marshmallows melt, a tasty show.
But oops! My mittens got stuck in the goo,
Now how am I supposed to eat my stew?

Footprints lead to the fridge, such a quest,
For midnight snacks, we need the best!
But sneaking treats hides a tricky trap,
A sleepy cat takes a cozy nap.

So let's wrap up this frosty spree,
With silly dreams and hot tea.
For when the dawn brings golden light,
We'll laugh again at the wondrous night.

Ebon Skies and Frosted Pines

An evening stroll through streets aglow,
With twinkling lights putting on a show.
I tripped on ice, did a little spin,
Thank goodness no one's nearby to grin.

Frosty air and banquet smells,
From grandma's kitchen, where joy dwells.
With cookies piled high and a cat that leaps,
She swipes a treat, then off she creeps!

The pines are dressed, all decked in white,
But there's a squirrel causing quite a fright.
He thinks he's Santa in disguise,
As he tumbles down from his lofty rise.

So gather round, let stories unfold,
Of winter nights and adventures bold.
For in this fun, we truly find,
Glee in the frosty tales combined.

Illusions of Warmth in the Cold

A mug of cocoa in my hand,
I thought it was a sunlit land.
But outside, penguins wave so grand,
While I search for my missing hand.

My socks are cozy, thick, and bright,
Yet I still shiver, what a sight!
The snowman laughs in pure delight,
As I pretend my scarf's just right.

I built a fort, I'm king, you see,
Till a flake lands on my knee.
The icicles, they taunt me—glee,
As I wonder, is this how it must be?

In blankets piled, I start to dream,
Of tropical shores, a sunny beam.
But pancakes stacked with whipped cream,
Wait, what's that? I just heard a scream!

Heartbeats in Frozen Air

Underneath my frozen hat,
I can't feel my nose—not that!
I try to dance, but slip and splat,
Laughter echoes, and that is that!

Footprints zigzag like a dance,
While I take my frosty chance.
The snowflakes fall as if in trance,
With feathery style, they enhance.

My breath, it puffs, a smoky plume,
A winter dragon starts to loom.
I chase it down the snowy zoom,
While winter's chill fills every room.

But here comes spring, in such a hurry,
Melting my dreams, don't make me worry!
I'll trade my snow pants for a flurry,
Of sunshine, warmth—oh what a flurry!

Beneath the Glare of Bone-white Skies

A snowball hits me, right on cue,
With laughter shared, my face turns blue.
The clouds above seem to construe,
A winter play, I'm acting too!

Icicles hang like teeth of beasts,
While snowmen feast on carrot feasts.
In frozen glee, we are the priests,
Of this cold church, where warmth is least.

I slip again, oh what a blunder,
While friends erupt in peals of thunder.
A snow angel formed, my body under,
Proving winter's never just a ponder.

As night falls down, I start to freeze,
But inside, I dream of summer's breeze.
With cookies warm and laughter, please,
Just let me roast some marshmallows with ease!

Nocturnal Dance with the Cold

The moon shines bright on icy ground,
I slip on black ice, and oh, I'm crowned!
A dance so silly, all around,
With laughter bouncing, joy unbound.

Snowflakes swirl, a fluffy trance,
As winter bids us all to dance.
I twirl and spin without a chance,
To stay upright, such a romance!

Each breath I take, a cloud appears,
Like tiny ghosts, they disappear.
I giggle loud, despite my fears,
While frosty critters lend me cheers.

The night grows silent, stars aglow,
Yet in this cold, I wave hello.
With laughter warm, we steal the show,
No need for blankets, we've got the flow!

Lantern Light in the Darkness

When the lantern flickers bright,
I dance like a silly sprite.
Snowflakes land on my nose,
As I try to strike a pose.

The shadows stretch and creep,
While laughter runs so deep.
I trip on ice, oh dear!
But giggles fill the air, not fear.

Shivering Shadows Under Stars

Beneath the stars so bold,
I wear my grandpa's old coat.
It's three sizes too big,
But it makes me dance a jig!

The moon looks down and grins,
As I fall, just like the sins.
Shadows flicker and hide,
While I giggle, heads collide.

Frostbite Serenade

I sing to the frost tonight,
With a voice that sure ain't right!
The icicles start to sway,
As I beatbox all the way.

My fingers freeze, I clap,
But oh, I take a nap!
A snowman laughs with glee,
As I snooze beneath a tree.

Silence Wrapped in Snow

Wrapped in silence, what a joke,
The dog just let out a yoke.
Snowball fights break the calm,
My aim, it feels like a bomb!

The cold has made us all bright,
In sweaters that feel just right.
With hot cocoa in hand,
We laugh and make snow angels in the land.

Gazing at the Shimmering Sky

Stars in pajamas, twinkle with glee,
I'm convinced they're laughing, just like me.
Facing the cold, I stomp my toes,
While dreaming of beaches, in fancy clothes.

Snowflakes giggle as they softly fall,
They dance like penguins, one and all.
I catch them on my tongue with delight,
And suddenly wish for a snowball fight!

Hot cocoa's waiting, a marshmallow throne,
Sipping it slow, I'm king on my own.
But I spilled some toppings, now it's a mess,
Life's little blunders, I guess I confess.

Footprints everywhere, all zigzag and wild,
A wintery Yeti? Or just my inner child?
With mittens on hands and a hat that's too tight,
I embrace the frost with all of my might.

Frost-Licked Thoughts of a Wandering Heart

Outside my window, the world's wearing frost,
I miss summer's warmth, but that dream's been lost.
The dog in his sweater, looks slightly confused,
His tail's wagging hard, he's thoroughly amused.

Neighbors are bundled in coats far too bright,
Sipping warm drinks in their cozy respite.
A snowman's been built, with a great big nose,
But his carrot got eaten; where did it go?

My thoughts wander off, like a kite in the sky,
Chasing fluffy clouds that seem oh so spry.
Ice on the pond looks like glassy mirage,
I hesitate to skate, fearing my barrage.

Yet here I am, bundled up, ready to roam,
Finding joy in the chill, this place feels like home.
With laughter, we gather, beneath all the flake,
And winter's a joke, life's a giggly mistake!

Waking the Night Frost

The night is alive with a magical cheer,
Frost tickles my nose, no need for a beer.
The moon pulls a prank, shining bright on my street,
While shadows do cha-cha on icy repeat.

I slip on a patch, my feet take a flight,
Doing an unusual dance in the night.
Laughter erupts as I land with a thud,
Could winter be just a comical flood?

My breath makes a cloud, like a dragon so bold,
Sharing secrets with stars, their stories untold.
Each silly snowflake demands to be caught,
But they all seem to vanish, where'd they all trot?

In this frosty kingdom, I'm ruler supreme,
Building up snow forts, living the dream!
And when I wake up, I'll smile in my bed,
With frozen adventures still dancing in my head.

A Canvas of White Beneath Silent Skies

A soft layer blankets the world in delight,
Nature's own canvas, pure, sparkling, bright.
Sidewalks are whispering secrets to toes,
As I try not to slip on the ice that still glows.

The sun peeks through, gives the snow a soft wink,
While my nose is redder than the bottle of drink.
A snowball is flying, my friend ducking low,
But my aim is a mess—does that count as a show?

Giggling children, with cheeks rosy and round,
In their frosty fort, they throw laughter all around.
They build little armies and watch them all fall,
A playful rebellion, oh, the joy in it all!

As the evening falls, we gather and cheer,
Hot stew in our bowls, what a toast to the year!
Winter's a lively, giggly delight,
Painting our hearts with its whimsical night.

Beneath the Icy Canopy

The trees are dressed in coats so white,
Squirrels slide down, what a silly sight!
Hot cocoa spills, oh dear, what a mess,
    I swear my toes are in a duress!

Penguins in hats, waddling with glee,
They dance like they're free, oh can't you see?
Snowmen gossip, their noses askew,
    "Who wore it better?" they giggle, it's true.

Fluffy flakes fall, landing on my nose,
I sneeze, and suddenly, the chaos grows!
A snowball flies, right into my face,
    Laughter erupts in this frosty place.

At night, the stars blink through the trees,
Dreaming of summer, the warm, gentle breeze.
But while we frolic, hot tea in hand,
    We smile at the snow, oh isn't it grand?

Winter's Whispering Lullaby

Underneath this soft, snowy quilt,
I slip on ice, oh, my pride is spilt!
The moon giggles as I take a slide,
Wishing for a chairlift to rescue my pride.

The breeze carries whispers of sneaky frost,
Dogs in sweaters, oh, they've really lost!
They prance and jump in the fluff so deep,
While I'm over here, trying not to weep.

Fireside stories of yetis and more,
"Who left the sleigh open?" I snicker and snore.
Grappling with mittens, fingers in a fight,
Tasting marshmallows, oh, what a delight!

But when all is quiet, and stars peek through,
I chuckle aloud, "What else can we do?"
With snowmen chatting and snowflakes free,
I embrace the night, in perfect glee.

Frosted Whispers of Twilight

Little bunnies hop in their fluffy coats,
Dodging my snowball like crafty little goats!
Frosted the windows, a drawing so sweet,
I'm lost in a battle with hot soup and feet.

Twilight brings glimmers of shimmering cheer,
As icicles dangle, I question my beer.
"Did you say 'cold?'" I hear my friend say,
But honestly, isn't this just a game we play?

With laughter that echoes amid frosted trees,
We wear our scarves, not just for degrees.
Yet while we pretend that we're all hardcore,
We dream of the tropics, next trip on the shore!

So here we are, with snowflakes that fall,
I chuckle at winter, it's all quite the ball.
While some shiver and cringe, I find my delight,
In these frosted whispers, oh what a night!

Silent Embrace of the Snowfall

Flakes dance down, like confetti they glide,
I leap outside, my boots are untied!
Sip on the chocolate that drizzles my chin,
Winter's parade, let the fun times begin!

Friends build a fortress, while wearing a grin,
A snowball lands, chaos sparks from within!
"Dodge to the left!" my buddy does yell,
And suddenly, I find myself in a shell.

Night falls gently, stars twinkle in glee,
While watching the glow, I trip on my knee!
We gather around, with tales full of cheer,
Tales of the snowman who's gone for a beer.

So here we are, wrapped in laughter and joy,
Creating sweet memories, oh boy, oh boy!
In the embrace of the night, we all will unite,
In a wintery wonder, so cozy and bright.

Frost-Kissed Whispers

The snowman wears a silly hat,
His carrot nose, a comical spat.
A penguin slips on frozen ground,
While laughter echoes all around.

The hot cocoa's extra sweet,
But spills make quite a frosty treat.
Snowflakes dance like frisky bees,
While we freeze, just hoping to sneeze!

Icicles hang like pointy teeth,
The winter's breath, a frozen sheath.
We bundle up like puffed-up birds,
And share our jokes, despite their flurbs.

As frost bites cheek and ear alike,
Here's to snowball fights and slippery bike!
Winter's whims make all things bright,
With giggles shared in the frosty light.

Beneath a Silver Veil

Beneath the moon's frosty shine,
Squirrels dress in outfits divine.
Trees wear coats of shimmering white,
While raccoons plot in the quiet night.

The shivering cat looks quite a sight,
Prowling around with all her might.
A jolly snowman, so proud and round,
Dances around without a sound.

The stars above begin to wink,
While neighbors argue over the clink.
Snowflakes fall like soft confetti,
On tangled hair, so very messy.

With mittens lost and scarves a-knock,
We'll have a laugh and check the clock.
For in this cold, we find our cheer,
With warmth in hearts and winter beer!

Echoes of Midnight Haze

The wind howls loud, a ghostly tune,
While folks in pajamas dance under the moon.
Snowballs fly, and giggles reign,
Each tumble yields a frosty gain.

A snowangel lies flopped in the snow,
With wild designs that steal the show.
Footprints lead to what we forgot:
The mittens, flung for a careless plot.

Cocoa spills, a delicious fail,
As marshmallows float like a ship's tail.
We laugh until our cheeks go red,
Warm hearts battle the frost ahead.

The clock strikes one, it's time for bed,
But who can sleep with fun instead?
So we whisper tales of snowman pride,
While cozy and bright, we snuggle inside.

Frosted Dreams at Dusk

The sky glows pink, the sun extends,
Snowflakes drift like gentle friends.
Funny hats adorn the crowd,
As we laugh, our spirits loud.

Polar bears in cozy socks,
And penguins sport their polar frocks.
Toboggans fly with a swoosh and a spin,
While giggly teens try to fit right in.

The cat's in a snowdrift, don't you see?
Wearing a scarf, a sight of glee.
With frosty breath, we share our tales,
Of snowman dances and silly fails.

As dusk arrives in a twinkling show,
And snowflakes fall with a playful flow,
We toast to nights of frosty fun,
With love and laughter for everyone!

Conversations with the Frosty Wind

I asked the breeze to tell me a joke,
It laughed so hard, it made me choke.
'Why did the snowman start to run?'
'He heard the sun was having some fun!'

I wrapped my scarf a little too tight,
The frost was tickling, what a sight!
'You call that a laugh? That's just a sneeze!'
'Try laughing instead, it'll put you at ease.'

The trees were giggling, branches all sway,
They whispered secrets of winter's play.
'Why are you stuttering, my frosty friend?'
'I'm just blown away, it's a chilly trend!'

So here I stand with my comic muse,
Frosty tales that I happily choose.
Laughter dances in the nippy air,
As I converse with the chill without a care.

The Bite of the Midnight Hour

When the clock struck twelve, what a bite it took,
With frozen toes, my warm self it shook.
I hopped and jived, the sheets felt a tease,
'Are you trying to chill me, or just freeze?'

An ice cream cone in my fridge did mock,
It whispered sweetly, 'Take me for a walk!'
'Out in the snow? You're completely bonkers!'
'Tell me that again, and you'll be my sponsor!'

The shadows danced like they wanted to play,
'Join us outside, lest you miss the fray!'
I chuckled deep, my breath a cloud,
'Not too loud now, or winter's too proud!'

So I shivered and snickered hand in hand,
With frostbitten laughter, I made my stand.
In the midnight hour, that nippy delight,
Had me chuckling in the heart of the night.

Stars Adrift on Arctic Air

Stars twinkled down with a frosty sigh,
Each one a gem in the night-sky high.
They whispered, 'Hey, do you feel that chill?'
'It's the joke of the night, so take a thrill!'

'Have you heard of the star that lost its shine?'
'It moved so fast, it crossed a line!'
I laughed so hard, the snowflakes danced,
It seems even they were caught in a trance.

A comet passed by with a comet's grin,
'Tell me, my friend, where have you been?'
'Chasing the sun and bursting with light,'
'But now I'm just floating — oh, what a sight!'

With stars adrift on the frosty breeze,
Each one chuckling, doing as they please.
So up I gazed, all worries went bare,
A cosmic comedy, high in the air.

Dreaming of Firelight

In my cozy room, the shadows play,
While outside the world is dark and gray.
I dream of fire, of warmth and dance,
But the frost just giggles at my romance.

The logs in the fireplace gave a sigh,
'Tell us a secret, don't just pass by!'
'What's the scoop on the snowflakes' spree?'
'They're having a party, come join and see!'

The floorboards creaked with a sly little wink,
'Keep those dreams warm, or they'll freeze, I think!'
I piled on blankets, each one a shield,
Against the jokes that the cold dared to field.

So here I recline, in my blanket fort,
Dreaming of embers, warmth is my sport.
For in frosty nights, a laugh I will find,
In dreams of firelight, joy intertwined.

Timeless Beauty in Winter's Grasp

Snowflakes swirl like dancers in the breeze,
Little kids bundle up, trying to squeeze.
Hot cocoa steaming, marshmallows afloat,
While Rudolph's nose glows, it plays peek-a-boat.

Frosty faces with hats far too large,
Snowmen grinning, they take charge.
Sledding down hills, oh what a sight,
Face-planting in snow—oh, what a fright!

Icicles hang like teeth in a grin,
Who knew the cold could bring such spin?
Turtlenecks fighting with scarves in a race,
Chasing warmth, we make goofy face.

So here's to the fun that this season can bring,
With laughter and joy, let the frosty bells ring.
No matter the freeze in the snowy parade,
We find our warmth in the games that we played.

Solitude Wrapped in Frost

The world outside wraps in a quiet white sheet,
Covered in blankets, we fight off the heat.
Sipping tea with a cat on our lap,
In solitude's hug, we'll take a long nap.

Pajamas mismatched, hair looking a fright,
Adventures include a run to the light.
Frosty windows, we peek through the glass,
Wishing the snowstorm would just let us pass.

Woolly socks slide across the floor,
Every glass shatters with a comical roar.
Eagerly waiting for dinner's great call,
Mismatched leftovers make quite the ball!

But when the fridge thaws and sends us away,
We tumble and trip, oh what a buffet!
So here's to the moments of laughter and cheer,
In solitude wrapped, we've nothing to fear.

Flickering Memories in Flurries

Dancing around in a frenzy of snow,
Scarf spinning wildly, oh where did it go?
Fingers are frozen on icy front doors,
But springs of laughter burst from our cores.

With snowballs exchanged like letters of old,
We craft silly stories that never grow cold.
Each flurry a spark, igniting our days,
Remembering moments in whimsical ways.

As shadows stretch long, the evening sets in,
Stories of snowmen with fabulous fins.
Tails of adventure unfold in the night,
As popcorn flies in an epic snow fight.

So gather your friends, let the memories flow,
In flickering fires, let our laughter grow.
While snowflakes drop rhythms on rooftops so dear,
We'll cherish these moments through every year.

Voices of the Winter Wind

Whispers of winter dance through the trees,
Tickling our ears with a chill on the breeze.
Sledding down mountains, we tumble and slide,
As the winter wind howls, we all run to hide.

Laughter erupts from beneath frosty hoods,
As parents return with overflowing goods.
A snowman debates with a polar bear hat,
Caught in a contest to see who's more fat.

Pine needles crackle, a chorus most sweet,
We waddle and bounce in our boots to the beat.
Icicles chime as they jingle and sway,
While snowflakes take turns to join in the play.

So here's to the voices that winter bestows,
In giggles and chatter, the fun only grows.
With a wink and a grin as we dance through the night,
We'll follow the wind, let our spirits take flight.

Comfort in the Snap of the Cold

Hot cocoa in my favorite mug,
Sock puppets dance, oh what a hug!
Blanket forts, we'll build them high,
As snowflakes tumble from the sky.

Mittens made of mismatched threads,
A snowball fight, we forge ahead.
My nose is pink, my laughter loud,
In this frosty, playful crowd.

Hot pies bubble, smell so sweet,
Polar bear socks on my cold feet.
Giggles burst like frozen treat,
Joy warms up the winter street.

Sipping soup as snowflakes land,
Joking 'bout our frozen hands.
This brisk breeze makes spirits soar,
With laughter echoing once more.

Melodies of Icy Whispers

In the backyard, snowmen grow,
They wear my hat; it's quite the show!
Carrot noses, smiles so wide,
Frosty friends we cannot hide.

Whispers of ice play on the wind,
Snowball jokes that never end.
We build a fort, a snowy dome,
Imagination finds a home.

Sledding down the hill with glee,
Who knew snow could be so free?
Giggles chasing, down we go,
Like little rabbits lost in snow.

Warm mittens swap for icy hands,
Then we slip on frozen lands.
Laughter rings, oh what a scene!
Winter fun, our snowy dream.

Frosted Branches Under a Quiet Sky

Trees adorned in crystal lace,
Nature's frosty, funny face.
Squirrels dart, with great delight,
Chasing each other in the night.

A snowflake lands upon my nose,
Surprise! It tickles, oh, it glows!
I try to catch them with my tongue,
Like childhood songs, forever sung.

Breath like smoke, we frolic fast,
Making memories that will last.
Friends bundled up, we share a cheer,
Wrapped in laughter, never fear!

Under stars that twinkle bright,
We share our giggles, pure delight.
The branches sway, with whispers low,
In this frosty, funny show.

Silence Wrapped in Icy Breeze

Softly drifts the white, sweet air,
Puffing cheeks, we do not care.
We dance around in beanie hats,
And play the game of "Who's the Brat?"

Snowflakes twirl like tiny fairies,
Popping up just like our dairies.
Fingers cold, but spirits high,
Like rubber ducks, we waddle by.

Staring up at the moonlit scene,
Hot chocolate spills, oh what a glean!
Marshmallows plop, oh what a fight,
Every drop a pure delight.

Kites of snow we fly and chase,
Sliding down with the silliest grace.
Wrapped in warmth, our laughter frees,
In this wonder of icy breeze.

Stars Caught in Icy Nets

Twinkling lights upon the ground,
Fallen stars—what a sight found!
They grin and giggle with delight,
Trapped in nets, oh what a night!

A cosmic game of hide and seek,
Stars ask, "Hey, did you peek?"
They shiver, teeth chattering with cheer,
"Catch us if you can, we're right here!"

The moon laughs with a frosty glow,
As they sparkle, putting on a show.
Ice slips by with a slippery grin,
"No ice here? Well, let the fun begin!"

A ruckus brewed from far and near,
Winter's punchline that we all cheer.
The stars escape in a flurry of light,
Laughing as they dance into the night!

An Evening of Shimmering Silence

A blanket quiet as a sleeping cat,
Sapphire skies where shadows chat.
Snowflakes waltzing, landing near,
Whispering secrets we can hear.

Snowmen plotting with frosty glee,
"Let's make it hard to find the key!"
In muffled mirth, they conspire tight,
To make every snowball a soft little fight!

Trees covered in icing, looking perplexed,
What's going on? They are vexed!
With every branch draped in white,
They sway in laughter, feeling just right.

Even the candles flicker and say,
"It's too cold to chase the day!"
Together they giggle under the moon,
Joking that spring won't come too soon!

Wandering Through the Hush of Night

Footprints in snow, a curious path,
Where laughter follows like a warm bath.
Each crunch of ice a silly tune,
Bouncing along like a festive balloon.

Frogs in mittens, cats in boots,
Silly animals in winter suits!
A penguin slides down for a laugh,
While the moon shakes its head, "Here's the gaffe!"

Snowflakes tumble, oh what a sight,
Chasing each other, oh what delight!
They tease and tumble, dance through the air,
As I trip and fall, no need to bear.

Whispers of whimsy float through the trees,
As dogs fashion sleds out of ease.
"Come join the fun, don't be shy,
You'll fall into laughter, oh me, oh my!"

Dreams Beneath the Ice

Under frozen reflections, dreams convene,
Dancing sparks in a winter sheen.
Penguins tap-dance while bears roll,
A jolly band on an icy stroll.

Bubbles of laughter pop like a tune,
As otters whizz by on a makeshift moon.
Getting cozy with their icy snack,
Looking for pizza under the pack!

"Do we serve chili?" the ice asks in jest,
"Or shall we make hot cocoa? That's the best!"
Sipping cocoa, the frost does a jig,
While chilly breezes play hide and gig.

Chattering squirrels with acorns galore,
Dress up to dance, oh what a chore!
Under the frozen stars so bright,
They spin and twirl into the night!

Echoes in the Empty Night

The moon is playing hide and seek,
While snowflakes dance and start to peek.
A squirrel wrapped in a fluffy coat,
Complains that winter's just a joke!

My fingers freeze upon my phone,
I text my friends, but I'm alone.
They laugh and tease from cozy nooks,
While I'm stuck reading frozen books.

A snowman grins with a carrot nose,
Its eyes are rocks from garden clothes.
With frosty breath, it seems to say,
'You're not as smart as me today!'

The stars above have frozen smiles,
While I wrap up in funky styles.
In winter's mischief, we find delight,
As we giggle at the frosty night.

Winter's Breath on Slumbering Souls

The blankets pile, yet still I freeze,
As winter whispers with a tease.
My tea goes cold; I start to pout,
A grumpy snore is all I shout!

Outside, the car is trapped in snow,
I swear it should've learned to go.
I wave at neighbors, lost in their boots,
While my dog thinks it's fun to hoot!

The icicles dangle, pulling pranks,
They drip on hats, and steal our thanks.
Each step I take, a slip and slide,
As winter giggles at my pride.

With cheeks like cherries, noses red,
We gather 'round to share our bread.
Through frosty windows, laughter's bright,
In every breath of frigid night.

Frosted Petals on Still Wind

A snowflake lands upon my nose,
It tickles me, then quickly goes.
My hair, like icicles, starts to sway,
I must look silly in this play!

The trees are dressed in frosty gowns,
While rabbits hop in muffled sounds.
With every bounce, they slide and spin,
Their antics make me grin and grin.

I lost my mitten in the drifts,
Where's it gone? Oh, winter's gifts!
The dog runs off with my lost glove,
I chase him down; it's true love.

With frosted petals on the breeze,
We dance and laugh, we take our ease.
While winter pulls its frosty shroud,
We're just two kids, still playing loud.

Secrets of the Snowy Embrace

Under blankets, secrets hide,
While snowflakes tumble, winter's pride.
A pillow fight turns into fluffs,
We're giggling loud, forget the gruffs.

The hot cocoa spills like the sun,
As I try to clean, it's more fun.
Marshmallows float, a sweet delight,
I'm in a war that feels just right!

My neighbor's snowman leans and sways,
I think he's had too many days.
With a wink and snowball that he throws,
We laugh as winter freely glows.

In every flake, a story spins,
Of snowball fights and winter wins.
We gather close, secret embrace,
In every laugh, winter's wild grace.

Lanterns in a Frozen Dream

Beneath the moon, we slip and slide,
Chasing snowflakes as they glide.
Hot cocoa spills, laughter bursts,
In frozen air, our joy immerses.

Snowmen wobble, hats askew,
Carrot noses, a winking view.
Snowball fights in mittened hands,
Snotty noses, youthful bands.

Icicles hang like frozen swords,
While snowmen make their frosty hoards.
In frozen breath, we weave a tale,
Of giggles caught in winter's gale.

When lanterns glow in frost-kissed trees,
We dance around, unbothered by freeze.
With cheeks so red, we shout and cheer,
A frosty night, what fun is here!

Shadows of Ice and Silence

In silent nights, the shadows creep,
Winter's secrets, oh so deep.
We don our hats that are two sizes too big,
And trip on flurries, a comedic jig.

There's a joy in slippery runs,
Fall and roll, who needs the fun?
Hot tea spills—just add some spice,
We chuckle loudly, oh how nice!

Footprints trace our laugh-filled trails,
Attempts at snow angels—oh, the fails!
With mittens wet and faces bright,
We celebrate this frosty night.

A snowman tells us silly jokes,
With a carrot grin, he surely pokes.
In sparkling white, the night takes flight,
Laughter dances through the starry light.

Frost Kisses on Midnight Skin

At midnight hour, we quilt the night,
Snug inside, we hold on tight.
Snowflakes tickle as they fall,
While we share secrets wrapped in shawl.

Missed a step? Oh, down we go!
Rolling 'round like flakes in tow.
We imitate penguins on the street,
As our chilly noses laugh and meet.

Frosty kisses, whispers bold,
In the night, our smiles unfold.
Around a fire, we share our dreams,
In winter's grip, how funny it seems!

Wearing layers—oh, what a sight!
A fashion show of humor bright.
Bundled up, we prance with glee,
This frozen life is pure jubilee!

Beneath a Blanket of Stars

Under blankets, we squish and fight,
For the best spot in the pale moonlight.
With snacks galore and giggles loud,
We own the night, oh, winter proud.

The stars above seem to wink and tease,
While we wrap up warm, as snug as peas.
Counting constellations, oh what a game,
How many can share our wacky name?

Frost-bitten toes, a ticklish thing,
With whispered jokes, we all take wing.
The night unfolds with a playful jest,
In the frigid air, we feel so blessed.

Gazing up at the glimmering skies,
With chuckles and warmth, our spirits rise.
Underneath this sparkly display,
Winter lounging—oh what a play!

The Dance of Frost and Silence

In the stillness, sleigh bells ring,
Socks on hands, making winter sing.
Snowflakes stumble, they trip and fall,
The ground is slippery, not safe at all.

Frosty breath like dragon's puff,
Hot cocoa spills, oh, isn't it tough?
Chasing snowmen, with carrot noses,
But they just melt, like fading roses.

A scarf that wraps like a twisty hug,
Wrapped around me, like a warm drug.
Funny how snow looks pure and white,
But hides a puddle that gives a fright.

Sledding sideways, we twirl with glee,
Until we land on a bumblebee!
Laughter dances in the frosty air,
Winter antics, without a care!

Wisps of Icy Magic

Nighttime's cloak with a glimmering sheen,
Brings snowball fights, both fun and mean.
Chasing shadows, we play hide and seek,
Getting lost in the snow, oh so bleak!

Icicles dangle, a treacherous sight,
One on my nose brings a chilly bite.
Snowflakes whisper secrets so dear,
But eating yellow snow? That's never clear!

A snowman winks, with a grin of coal,
Watch him wobble, oh what a toll!
With every shove, he gives a shake,
A dance of laughter, make no mistake.

Sliding down slopes on patches of ice,
Hilarity strikes, like rolling dice.
A stumble, a tumble, no time for frowns,
Just winter giggles in puffy gowns!

Crystal Shadows on Mossy Ground

Pine trees shimmer, dressed in white,
Their branches shake, oh what a sight!
Snowy squirrels leap, with lofty grace,
Struggling to fit in their fluffy space.

Glistening frost on the grass so green,
Looks like diamonds, oh so serene.
But when I step, with a squelch and a slip,
I find myself in a muddy dip!

Hot chocolate spills, a surprise attack,
As we laugh on the floor, there's no turning back.
Snowball skirmishes, oh, what a mess,
Covered in snow, we giggle, no less.

We dance with shadows, under streetlight beams,
Creating mischief, fulfilling our dreams.
For the night is young and full of cheer,
With frosty faces and laughter to hear!

Embracing the Night's Cold Caress

Stars like sprinkles on a frosted cake,
We race like penguins, for goodness' sake.
Hot soup warming both hands, so tight,
While giggling snowflakes take off in flight.

A snow angel lies, but with a twist,
A belly flop—was that a miss?
With mittened hands, we mold and play,
Until the chilly night steals our stay.

Muffler wrapped tight, but it slips away,
I chase it down, what a clumsy display!
As if winter knows all my silly schemes,
And douses my fun with icy streams.

But who can resist the sparkling sight?
Of snowflakes dancing in the moonlight.
So let's embrace this playful show,
With hearts as warm as the fires we know!

Icy Echoes of Forgotten Dreams

When snowflakes dance with gleeful delight,
The cats in pajamas prepare for a fight.
A snowman winks with a carrot for a nose,
While icy winds play silly, tickling toes.

The cocoa spills over in frothy delight,
As marshmallows float like soft clouds in flight.
A snowball is launched with a giggle and glee,
But it hits a wise owl perched up in a tree.

Toot! Toot! The horn from a sled down the hill,
As neighbors come out, what a sight, what a thrill!
With laughter echoing through frostbitten air,
The night plays tricks, giving frostbite a scare.

So gather 'round fires, tell stories that shine,
Of penguins wearing tuxedos and wine.
For under the stars, where the moon's glow is bright,
We share silly whispers in the frosty night.

Enigmas of a Frostbitten Hearth

A fire crackles with a curious sound,
As squirrels in tuxedos queue up all around.
The stockings are stuffed with mischief and cheer,
While marshmallows laugh as they melt without fear.

Outside the window, a snowman is stuck,
He lost his right arm and ran out of luck.
The peppermint candy canes dance on their own,
While the reindeers complain of the frost on their bone.

The cat takes a leap, aimed for the warm bed,
But lands in the ashes, now fluffy and red.
A chorus erupts, from the laughter they bring,
As gingerbread cookies begin to do a jig.

So snuggle in tight, with your blankets galore,
Watch shadows that prance on the cold wooden floor.
With friends all around, oh the wonders tonight,
Unraveling enigmas in the firelight.

Frost-Draped Reflections

The moonlight glimmers on the frosty panes,
While squirrels on skates play their wintery games.
A family of penguins slide down the street,
In search of good snacks that are spicy and sweet.

Under tall pines draped in powdery white,
The elves come out dancing, oh such a sight!
With mittened hands, they spin with delight,
While snowflakes create a most whimsical flight.

The shadows of pines seem to come alive,
As snowmen start plotting how best to survive.
With carrots as swords and laughter on cue,
They march through the night, oh, what will they do?

So sip on your cocoa, let the giggles flow,
For under the frost, there's a magical show.
Where reflections of joy twinkle brightly and bold,
And the warmth of a laugh beats the frostbite so cold.

Glistening Secrets of the Night

A blanket of stars on the world's frosty face,
While raccoons in boots find the perfect place.
The whispers of night are a giddy delight,
As snowflakes tickle the noses in flight.

Jingle bells ring from afar with a cheer,
While penguins join in for the dance of the year.
With spirits so bright, they slip and they glide,
And soon all the critters join in for the ride.

The fox wears a scarf, so dapper and neat,
And fetches a hat for the penguins to greet.
As snowdogs zoom past with a wink and a bark,
They race under moonlight, the night's sweetest arc.

With giggles resounding in this snowy delight,
We hug our hot cocoa under swirls of the night.
For each frozen moment that's filled with good cheer,
Holds secrets of laughter, the magic so near.

Milton Keynes UK
Ingram Content Group UK Ltd.
UKHW022010131124
451149UK00013B/1096